WOMEN AND WAR

# THE SOVIET NIGHT WITCHES

## Brave Women Bomber Pilots of World War II

by Pamela Dell

CAPSTONE PRESS
a capstone imprint

**Snap Books are published by Capstone Press,**
**1710 Roe Crest Drive, North Mankato, Minnesota 56003**
**www.mycapstone.com**

Library of Congress Cataloging-in-Publication Data
Names: Dell, Pamela, author.
Title: The Soviet night witches : brave women bomber pilots of World War II /by Pamela Dell.
Description: North Mankato, Minnesota : Snap Books/Capstone Press, 2018. |
Series: Women and war | Includes bibliographical references and index.
Identifiers: LCCN 2017015336| ISBN 9781515779384 (library binding) | ISBN 9781515779452 (paperback) |
ISBN 9781515779490 (PDF)
Subjects: LCSH: World War, 1939-1945—Aerial operations, Soviet—Juvenile literature. |
Bomber pilots—Soviet Union—History—Juvenile literature. | Women air pilots—Soviet Union—History—
Juvenile literature. | Night flying—Soviet Union—History—Juvenile literature. | Soviet Union.
Voenno-Vozdushnye Sily—History—World War, 1939–1945—Juvenile literature. | World War, 1939–1945—Women—
Soviet Union—Juvenile literature.
Classification: LCC D792.S65 D455 2018 | DDC 940.54/4947082—dc23

LC record available at https://lccn.loc.gov/2017015336

Editorial Credits:
Megan Atwood, editor; Veronica Scott, designer; Jo Miller, media researcher

Photo Credits:
Alamy: AF Fotografie, 25, Andrew Kitching, cover, 5 (top), SPUTNIK, 6, 8 (bottom), 10, 12, 17, 24, 26; Getty Images:
Mansell, 21, Sovfoto, 22, TASS, 15, 27 (bottom); Newscom: akg-images, 18, Sovfoto Universal Images Group, 13;
Shutterstock: Ivan Cholakov, 5 (bottom), Militarist, 27 (top), Voinau Pavel, 9, 11; Wikimedia: Bundesarchiv, Bild 146-
1997-041-03 / CC-BY-SA 3.0, 7, unknown, 8 (top)

Design Elements: Shutterstock: Allexxandar, Eky Studio, udra11

Printed and bound in Canada.
010395F17

# TABLE OF CONTENTS

# Chapter 1

# SILENT AND DEADLY

On a dark night during World War II
(1939–1945), a small airplane takes flight.
Inside sits a Soviet pilot. Behind the pilot sits the
navigator. The navigator's job is to keep the plane on
course as the pilot flies over the Russian countryside.

The Soviets fly low. They are searching for enemy
facilities and hunting for German military camps and
supply storehouses. The pilot and navigator are on a
combat mission to destroy these sites. This is their
only chance. The plane they fly carries a payload of
just two bombs.

In the darkness below, an enemy target comes into
view. The Soviet plane cuts its engine, gliding almost
silently toward its mark. It beams no light. The Nazis
have no idea the Soviets are about to attack.

The Soviet plane moves in undetected. Its only
noise now is a soft whooshing sound. Once in
position for the drop, the pilot releases a single bomb.
The bomb makes a direct hit. In a sudden fiery flash,
the Nazi facility explodes.

The Night Witches have struck again.

# FACT

Nazi Germany launched Operation Barbarossa against the Soviet Union on June 22, 1941. It was an early and aggressive act of war. Millions of German enemy forces marched into the Union of Soviet Socialist Republics, or USSR (also called the Soviet Union). Operation Barbarossa remains the largest military invasion in the history of warfare.

The Soviet Union's Night Witches had a more official name: the 588th Night Bomber Regiment. The regiment was unique among all the Soviet air forces. This was not because of their unusual planes, and not because the planes carried only two bombs at a time. The regiment was unique because of its members: all of them were women. And they were all skilled, daring, and courageous.

The Night Witches trained hard to be in the Soviet military.

Throughout World War II, the 588th Regiment flew thousands of missions. They flew at night, in all weather conditions. Their aim was to attack the many German forces that were invading the USSR. The women dropped thousands of tons of bombs to combat the forces. Their bravery and successes made them heroes in the Soviet Union. They struck terror in the hearts of German soldiers.

# The Nachthexen

The German soldiers despised and feared the relentless 588th Regiment. They dreaded the soft, nearly silent swishing noise as the women's planes glided near. The planes' *whoosh-whoosh-whoosh* sound, heard only in the dead of night, reminded the men of a witch's broom, calling forth memories of frightening fairytales. It was the Germans who gave these women their legendary nickname. In German they were called *Nachthexen.* In English they were the "Night Witches."

"We simply couldn't grasp that the Soviet airmen that caused us the greatest trouble were in fact women. These women feared nothing. . . ."
— *Hauptmann Johannes Steinhoff,*
*German Commander of II./JG 52, September 1942*

# WOMEN ON A MISSION

In October 1941, USSR leader Joseph Stalin sent an official order to a well-known 29-year-old aviator. The aviator was Marina Raskova, a major in the Soviet Air Forces. She had persuaded Stalin that female combat pilots should join the war effort. His order commanded her to find and train these pilots.

There would be three women's regiments: the 586th Fighter Regiment, the 587th Day Bomber Regiment, and the 588th Night Bomber Regiment. Each regiment had at least 400 members. That number included pilots and navigators. It also included ground crew and mechanics.

Joseph Stalin

Marina Raskova

**FACT**

The Night Witches were sometimes called "Stalin's Falcons."

8

Flight training began in early 1942. It took place at an air base in Engels, a city on the Volga River in Russia. Thousands of young women from all over the USSR applied. Their average age was 22. Many were teenagers as young as 17. No one was older than 26. Most wanted to be pilots. But they all wanted to do their part against the Axis powers.

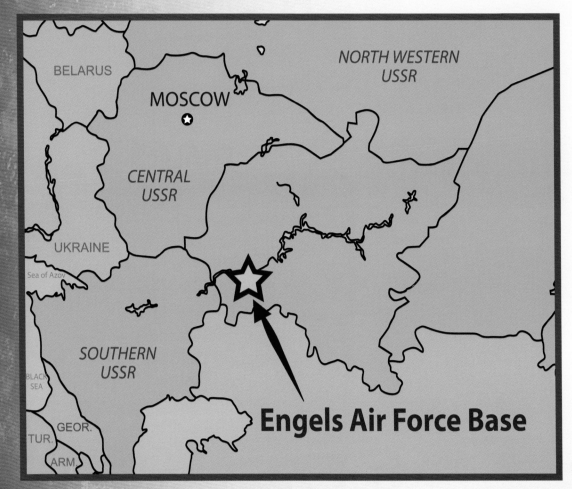

Engels Air Force Base

Most of the applicants were assigned to jobs on the ground crew or as mechanics. These positions were demanding. The women often worked outside in the worst weather, lifting and carrying heavy equipment. But their jobs were crucial for keeping the planes in good shape, both on the ground and in the air

Major Raskova chose only the most skilled pilots and navigators for the flight teams. She also personally oversaw their training. It was a big responsibility. Well-known pilots were celebrities in Soviet Russia. Raskova's young trainees felt honored to be commanded by a "Hero of the Soviet Union." But Raskova knew that many of them, no matter how good, would die in combat.

Marina Raskova, Polina Osipenko, and Valentina Grizodubova

## FACT

Combat flying was a risky business for the Soviets, men and women alike. By war's end more than 25 percent of the 588th Regiment had died in battle. From the beginning, Raskova tried to warn hopeful applicants of the dangers they would face in air combat. At one training session she asked them, "Aren't you frightened . . .? Don't you know these bad men on the other side will be shooting at you?" From the crowd came a loud reply: "Not if I shoot them first, Major Raskova!"

# The Russian Amelia Earhart

In May 1932, U.S. pilot Amelia Earhart became the first woman to fly solo across the Atlantic Ocean. She was not quite 35 years old. Like Earhart, Marina Raskova was the bravest of pilots. In 1938, at only 26 years old, she set a world record for long distance flight.

Along with two other women, Raskova flew almost 3,700 miles (6,000 kilometers) nonstop. Their flight took them from Moscow all the way to a city at the southeastern tip of Siberia, Komsomolsk-on-Amur. Near the end of their journey poor visibility took the women off-course.

Lost and running out of fuel, they prepared for an inevitable crash landing. Because a crash would mean certain death for navigator Raskova, who sat in the plane's nose, she bailed out. The other women flew on and later did crash but both survived. Raskova wandered the Siberian forest in search of her plane. She survived ten days with barely any food or water before finally reaching the crash site. All three women were rescued.

Back in Moscow Raskova and her two companions were celebrated. They became the first women to win the "Hero of the Soviet Union" medal. This was the highest honor in the USSR. Raskova died in January 1943 at 30 years old. Her plane crashed in a snowstorm as she tried to land. She was given the first state funeral of World War II.

In 1938 Marina Raskova and two other women flew nonstop from Moscow to Komsomolsk-on-Amur, some 3,672 miles (5,909 km) in 26 hours, 29 minutes.

# Chapter 3

# RISKY RIDES

The Night Witches risked death on a nightly basis. Their planes, hardly the best in the military, put the women at a dangerous disadvantage. They flew a simple type of two-seater aircraft called the Polikarpov Po-2. These 1920s-era planes had been mainly used for training. They were the slowest aircraft in the Soviet air forces. Now they were going into combat.

These small, low-flying planes were flimsy constructions of canvas and plywood. They were not covered in protective metal, and they had no radios, making communication with the ground impossible. Regular military aircraft carried radar to show the navigators where they were going. But the Po-2 navigators had nothing but compasses and maps.

The planes carried two bombs that hung beneath the plane wings. The cockpits were open to the weather. That meant the women were exposed to harsh cold and brutal winds. On winter flights, frostbite became another hazard.

Po-2 bomb being installed.

"When the wind was strong, it would toss the plane. In winter,
when you'd look out to see your target better, you got frostbite.
Our feet froze in our boots, but we carried on flying."

– Nadia Popova, 588th Regiment squad commander

ПАРТИЗАН

## FACT

Before the war, the Po-2 planes had
been used for a very different purpose.
Their job was to fly over farmland and
spray crops with chemicals to keep
insects away. So these aircraft were
often referred to as "crop dusters."

Things on the ground were not perfect either. From the beginning, the women of the 588th Regiment faced many obstacles and disadvantages. For one, the male soldiers resented the women's regiments. They bullied and ridiculed the women. Many men believed women should not be allowed to go into combat.

The clothes the women had to wear were also a problem. The Soviet military gave them oversized, badly fitting men's uniforms and even men's underwear. No matter their foot size, the only boots the women got were a men's size 42. And they were not allowed to wear perfume.

> "No one in the armed services wanted to give women the freedom to die."
>
> – Nadia Popova, 588th Regiment squad commander

Hair presented yet another problem. The male base commander at Engels ordered haircuts for all the women. Long, girlish locks were not "soldierly," he said. No one could have hair longer than 2 inches (5.1 centimeters). This was a big shock to many of the women. Traditionally, Russian women wore their hair long. Some wore braids. Others let their hair hang down their backs. But now it all had to go. The women of the 588th Regiment did not resist. They wanted to fly more than they wanted their hair. The day after the order, they all came to work with crewcuts.

Despite these orders, women maintained a strong sense of themselves in other ways. Many used the red navigational pencils to color their lips. They also painted flowers on their aircraft. The Witches were up for the challenge.

Soviet pilots of the 588th Regiment examine a fashion magazine during break time.

## FACT

When violent winds blew, grounded Po-2s were in danger. Sometimes, the mechanics had to lie flat on the lightweight planes' wings. The women's weight was the only thing that kept the planes from blowing away.

# DANCING WITH DEATH

Many women accepted into the 588th Regiment were already experienced pilots and navigators. The Soviet interest in aviation had increased greatly in the 1930s, and as part of this development, a network of "flying clubs" had been formed. Open to both men and women, these clubs were where many of the Night Witches first learned to fly. But they had never flown combat missions. This training would be a whole new experience.

Raskova rotated the flight teams. She had the pilots fly with different navigators. This helped her decide which two women worked best together.

Flight training was quick and intense. At the beginning of the war, the Germans had far fewer fighter pilots than the Soviets, but the Germans out-maneuvered their enemies because of their vastly superior flying skills. The Soviets could waste no time trying to equal them. In six months the women learned what normally took two years or more. They trained more than 12 hours a day to make this goal.

"Almost every time, we had to sail through
a wall of enemy fire."

– Nadia Popova, 588th Regiment squad commander

One important skill the women learned was "dogfighting." A dogfight was a battle in the air between two enemy aircraft flying close together. The women practiced dogfighting with each other. They also staged dogfights against their instructors. In these fake battles, a training team sometimes beat their teachers. This was always a thrill for the women.

## Tough as Nails

The female flight crews had a dangerous job. But their ground crews had a physically grueling one, especially the armorers--the women who loaded the planes' ammunition. When a plane returned from a mission, the armorers had as few as three to five minutes to load the next round of bombs for another attack. They had to lift the bombs out of crates to set the fuses. Then they attached the bombs, each weighing 220 pounds (100 kilograms), beneath the plane. An armorer might heft as much as three tons' worth of bombs in a single night. Meanwhile, other ground crew checked the mechanicals and did the refueling. Every member of every regiment was vital!

On their first mission, the Night Witches got an unexpected surprise. They were supposed to be escorted by larger Soviet aircraft. The women's planes carried no guns. So if Germans attacked, the escorts would defend the Po-2s.

Fearless flyers examine their planes.

But on this first flight, the commanders had another idea. They ordered the escorts to fake an attack on the Po-2s. The commanders wanted to see how the new combat pilots would do.

They did not do well. When attacked, the inexperienced women panicked. Thinking a real enemy was after them, they scattered.

Back on the base, their flying skills were praised. But when the women pilots discovered the truth, they were embarrassed. They vowed to prove how much courage they really had.

The proof came with the regiment's first bombing raid. That night, June 8, 1942, three planes were sent together on a mission. Their target was a German command post. This time their escorts really were there to protect them. The women flew through enemy gunfire to drop their bombs, never losing their nerve. One of their planes was destroyed and its crew killed. But the bombs had hit their target, and the other two planes returned safely. The Night Witches were on their way to glory.

# FACT

The women flying Po-2 planes were not issued parachutes until 1944. Before that, if a plane got in trouble, it usually meant death for the pilot and navigator.

The Night Witches mastered many daring moves. One of their main tasks was harassment bombing. This meant making surprise attacks in the middle of the night. And not just one attack, but many. The targets included German airfields, encampments, and other important facilities within Soviet territory.

The small, lightweight Po-2 planes had one big advantage. They were nimble. A pilot could make sudden decisive moves. Their planes could swoop, turn, and dive much more quickly than the Germans' bigger planes could. This made it easier to stay out of the enemy's way.

The Night Witches had one especially sneaky tactic. Three planes would go out together. Two would head for the target. Soon German searchlights on the ground would pick them out. The two planes would then shoot off in opposite directions.

While the searchlights tried to keep them in sight, the third plane went into action. Sneaking in under cover of darkness, that team would bomb the target. Then the three planes would regroup for another attack. Each time, a different plane would drop its payload. When all six bombs had been delivered, the Soviet squadron flew home. The Night Witches had a talent for outwitting the Nazis.

> "They came night after night in their very slow biplanes, and for some periods they wouldn't give us any sleep at all."
>
> — Hauptmann Johannes Steinhoff, German Commander of II./JG 52, September 1942

# The Night Witches Strike Again

Harassment bombing was dangerous. It was nerve-racking. But some nights it went on and on. The women made anywhere from 5 to 18 runs a night. Often they'd return in aircraft riddled with bullets.

Harassment bombing had another purpose besides hitting military targets. The constant attacks kept the German soldiers awake and on edge all night. The exhausted soldiers had no idea when the Witches would strike next.

Pilots planning an attack.

" . . . [the Germans'] barracks were built all in a neat row, and we would come at night, after they were asleep, and bomb them. Of course, they would have to run out into the night in their underwear . . . "

– *Galina Pavlovna Brok, member of the 588th Regiment.*

# Chapter 5

# HEROINES OF WAR

On October 25, 1942, the Night Witches struck a blow that went down in history. They targeted an enemy fuel station and airfield where seven German aircraft were parked. The bombs they dropped caused a fire that spread quickly. In the end, six of the seven aircraft were unusable.

This loss forced the Germans to retreat from the area, allowing the Soviets to gain important ground near Russia's Taman Peninsula. This was part of a conflict called the Battle of the Caucasus.

Battle of the Caucasus

By June 1942, the Night Witches' regiment had become part of the 46th Guard Night Bomber Aviation Regiment. Half a year later, on January 6, 1943, their brave service in the Caucasus conflict was officially recognized. They had shared in the Soviet victories at Taman Peninsula. To honor this achievement their regiment was renamed once again. They became the 46th Taman Guards Night Bomber Aviation Regiment. They continued flying missions throughout the war, doing so proudly under this name.

## Witches Brew?

Were the Night Witches superhuman? Some in Nazi Germany's air force, the Luftwaffe, might have thought so. The Luftwaffe was the world's most powerful air force. But Soviet women, they said, could see as well as cats in the dark. The Germans suspected they took pills or were given shots to improve their eyesight.

Nadezhda (Nadia) Popova, one of the most successful members of the Night Witches, knew better. "This was nonsense," she said later in life. "What we did have were clever, educated, very talented girls."

Long before the war ended, the Night Witches had more than earned one prize they wanted and deserved — the respect of their male comrades. Their skills had spoken for themselves.

By war's end, the Night Witches had an outstanding record. They had flown at least 23,672 missions. Each of them had flown 1,000 missions or more. Some reports estimate they dropped 23,000 tons (21,000 metric tons) of bombs. Only 30 members were killed in action. Of the survivors, 23 received the Hero of the Soviet Union medal. This was the highest honor in the USSR. Theirs was also the most decorated female regiment in the Soviet air forces. Today their legend lives on.

**FACT**

At the peak of its strength, the Night Bombers Regiment included 40 two-person crews.

The 587th Bomber Aviation Regiment

# Nadia Popova

One of the best known of the Night Witches was Nadia Popova. She joined the 588th Regiment early, and rose to become a deputy commander.

Nadia was fearless and determined. She was patriotic. But she also had a personal purpose in going to war. Her brother Leonid had been killed by the Germans only a year into the war. Later, the Nazis took over her family's home to use as a police station. Nadia wanted revenge.

And revenge she got. She fearlessly flew 852 missions—at one time making 18 runs in a single night. "We had an enemy in front of us," she once said, "and we had to prove that we were stronger and more prepared."

Nadia also had great good luck. She was shot down several times, but she always survived. After one successful mission, her plane was full of bullet holes. So were her helmet and the navigator's map. Nadia was unconcerned and told her navigator, "Katya, my dear, we will live long." This was true. Nadia Popova died on July 8, 2013, at age 91.

## FACT

The Hero of the Soviet Union medal was not Nadya Papov's only award. She also earned the Order of Lenin, the Gold Star, and the Order of the Red Star. All were prestigious Soviet awards.

# Chapter 6

# NOT FORGOTTEN

The 46th Night Bombers Regiment is long gone now. But the Night Witches are not forgotten. Books have been written about them. Several movies have been made. Their heroism is still an inspiration for young women.

After the war, the women of the 46th had to adjust to a new, "quieter" life. The stress of combat was over. A few, like Nadia Popova, continued flying. She also trained new pilots. But most had to return to the more traditional roles of the time. They stopped flying and became housewives and mothers. Some of the other women went on to new kinds of work. They took jobs in factories, farms, and other places.

Marina Raskova with her daughter, Tanya

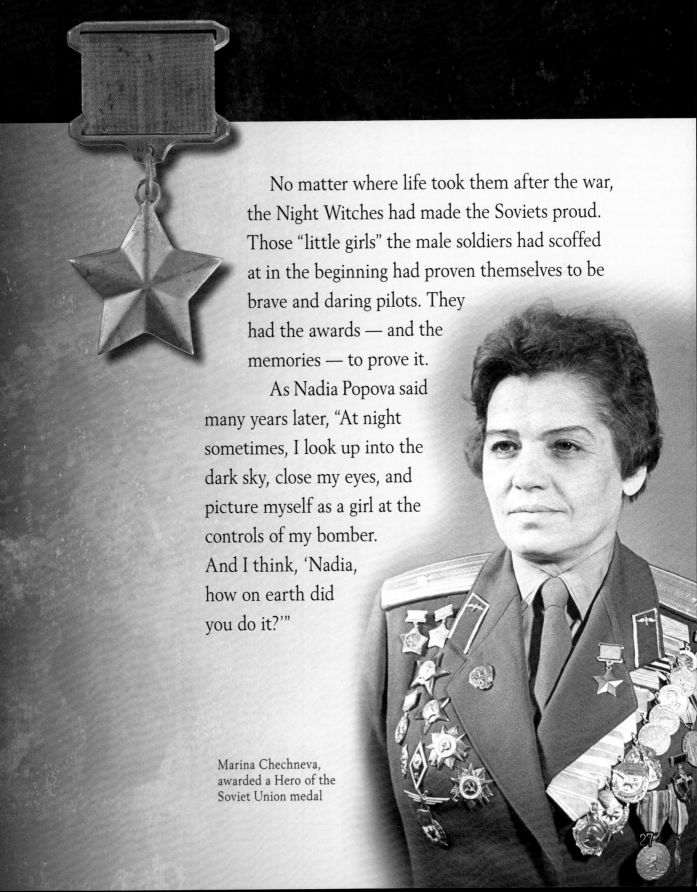

No matter where life took them after the war, the Night Witches had made the Soviets proud. Those "little girls" the male soldiers had scoffed at in the beginning had proven themselves to be brave and daring pilots. They had the awards — and the memories — to prove it.

As Nadia Popova said many years later, "At night sometimes, I look up into the dark sky, close my eyes, and picture myself as a girl at the controls of my bomber. And I think, 'Nadia, how on earth did you do it?'"

Marina Chechneva, awarded a Hero of the Soviet Union medal

# TIMELINE

## 1933

Marina Raskova becomes the first Soviet woman to pass the aviation exam and is licensed as a pilot.

## 1938

Raskova makes her record-breaking and death-defying flight across the Soviet Union to Siberia.

## June 1941

Soviet Union officially enters World War II.

## October 1941

Joseph Stalin orders the formation of three all-women air combat units. Among these is Regiment 588, nicknamed the Night Witches. One thousand women head to Engels, Russia, to begin training under the direction of Raskova.

## June 8, 1942

The Night Witches make their first bombing run.

## July 17, 1942 – February 2, 1943

The Soviet army successfully defends the city of Stalingrad (now Volgagrad) against the enemy. This battle kept the Germans from moving deeper into the Soviet Union and became the turning point in the war--bringing success to the Allies.

## December 9, 1942

Some squads from the 588th are commanded to stop the approach of an enemy ferry crossing the Terek River. The Germans spotlight one plane and shoot out its cockpit but the female pilot and navigator survive.

## January 4, 1943

Marina Raskova dies in a flight accident.

## July 31, 1943

Four of the Night Witches' planes are shot down by enemy fire.

## Early 1944

Three women are honored with medals as Heroes of the Soviet Union. By war's end, 23 of the Night Witches had earned this award.

## September 2, 1945

Japan surrenders, ending World War II.

## October, 1945

Now known as the 46th Taman Guards Night Bomber Aviation Regiment, the Night Witches are released from duty.

## July 8, 2013

Nadia Popova, one of the bravest and most celebrated Night Witches, dies in Moscow, Russia, at age 91.

# Glossary

**aviator** [AY-vee-ay-tor]—a pilot

**Axis powers** [ACK-sis POW-uhrs]—the enemy nations, which included Germany, Japan, and Italy

**bailed out** [BAYLD OWT]—jumped out

**combat** [com-BAT]—fighting between two or more forces

**compass** [CUHMP-uhs]—an instrument with an arrow that shows which direction is north

**decorated** [DECK-o-ray-tid]—awarded medals

**harassment** [ha-RAS-mehnt]—aggressive unwanted actions

**mission** [MI-shun]—an important job or assignment

**Nazi** [NAHZ-ee]—during WWII, a member of the Nationalist Socialists German Workers' political party

**nimble** [NIM-buhl]—movement that is light and quick

**payload** [PAY-lohd]—all the bombs an aircraft carries

**prestigious** [PRES-tee-juhs]—highly respected

**radar** [RAY-dahr]—electronic equipment for determining an aircraft's or ship's location, speed, and direction of travel. From the name RAdio Detection And Ranging

**regiment** [REHJ-uh-mehnt]—a military unit made up of many sections

**Soviet** [SOH-vee-et]—having to do with the former Union of Soviet Socialist Republics, or Soviet Union

**squadron** [SKWAH-druhn]—an air force unit that includes two or more aircraft and the people who fly them

**tactic** [TACK-tick]—an action planned to get specific results

# Read More

**Baker Moore, Shannon.** *Women with Wings: Women Pilots of WWII.* Minneapolis, Minn.: Essential Library, 2016.

**Burgan, Michael.** *World War II Pilots.* North Mankato, Minn.: Capstone Press, 2013.

**Rose, Simon.** *The Split History of World War II.* North Mankato, Minn.: Compass Point Books, 2016.

# Internet Sites

Use FactHound to find Internet sites related to this book.

Here's all you do:
Visit *www.facthound.com*

Just type in 9781515779384 and go.

# Critical Thinking Questions

1. What disadvantages did the women face as they worked to become part of the Soviet regiments? Point to places in the text that show this.

2. What sorts of things did the women do that showed how brave they were? Find instances in the text.

3. Discuss some examples of cause and effect found in the text. For example, what was the effect on male Soviet soldiers of women joining their ranks? Find other examples of how one event or action triggered another.

# Index